Fantastic ANIMALS

GRAYSCALE COLORING BOOKS

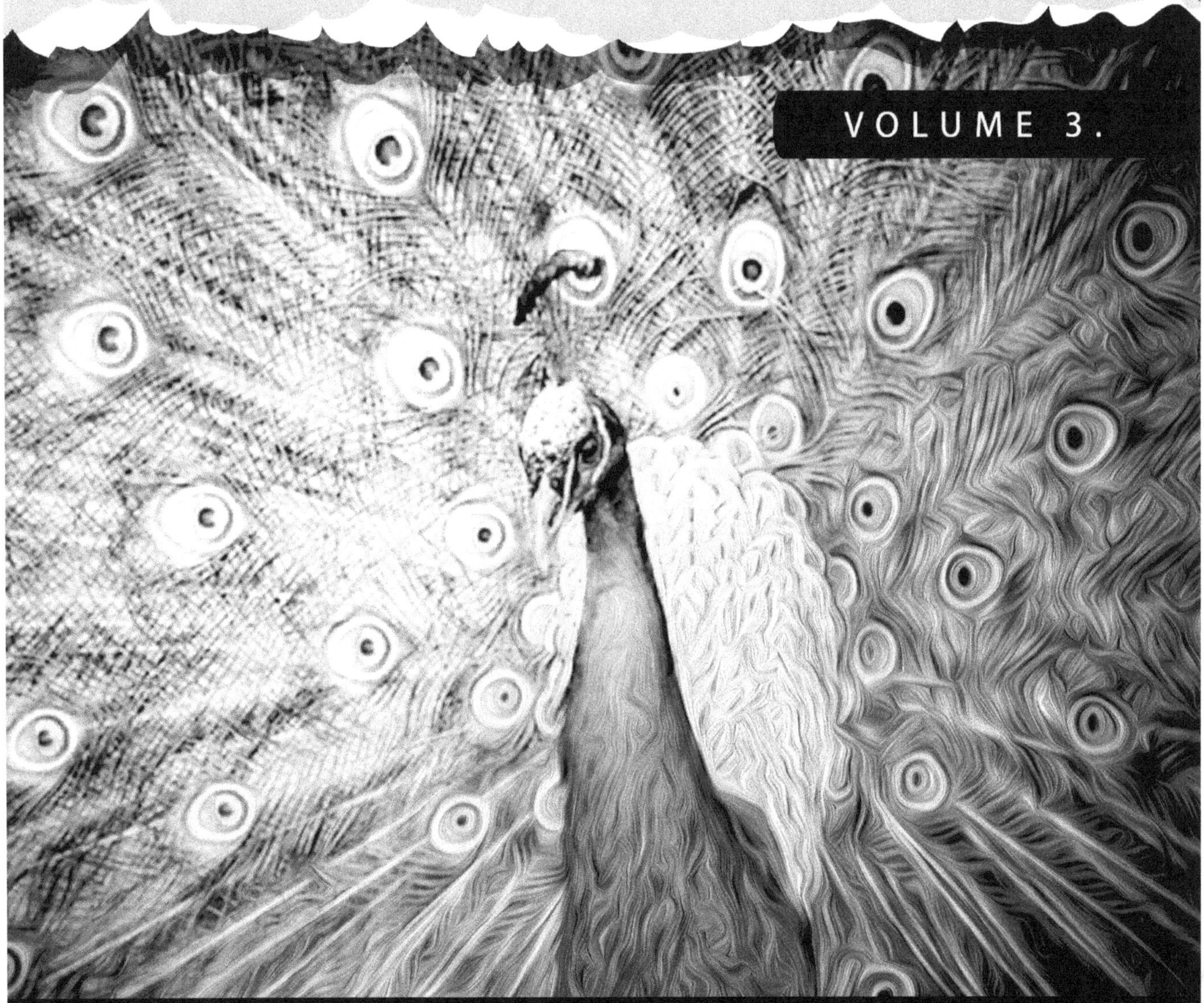

COLOR TEST PAGE

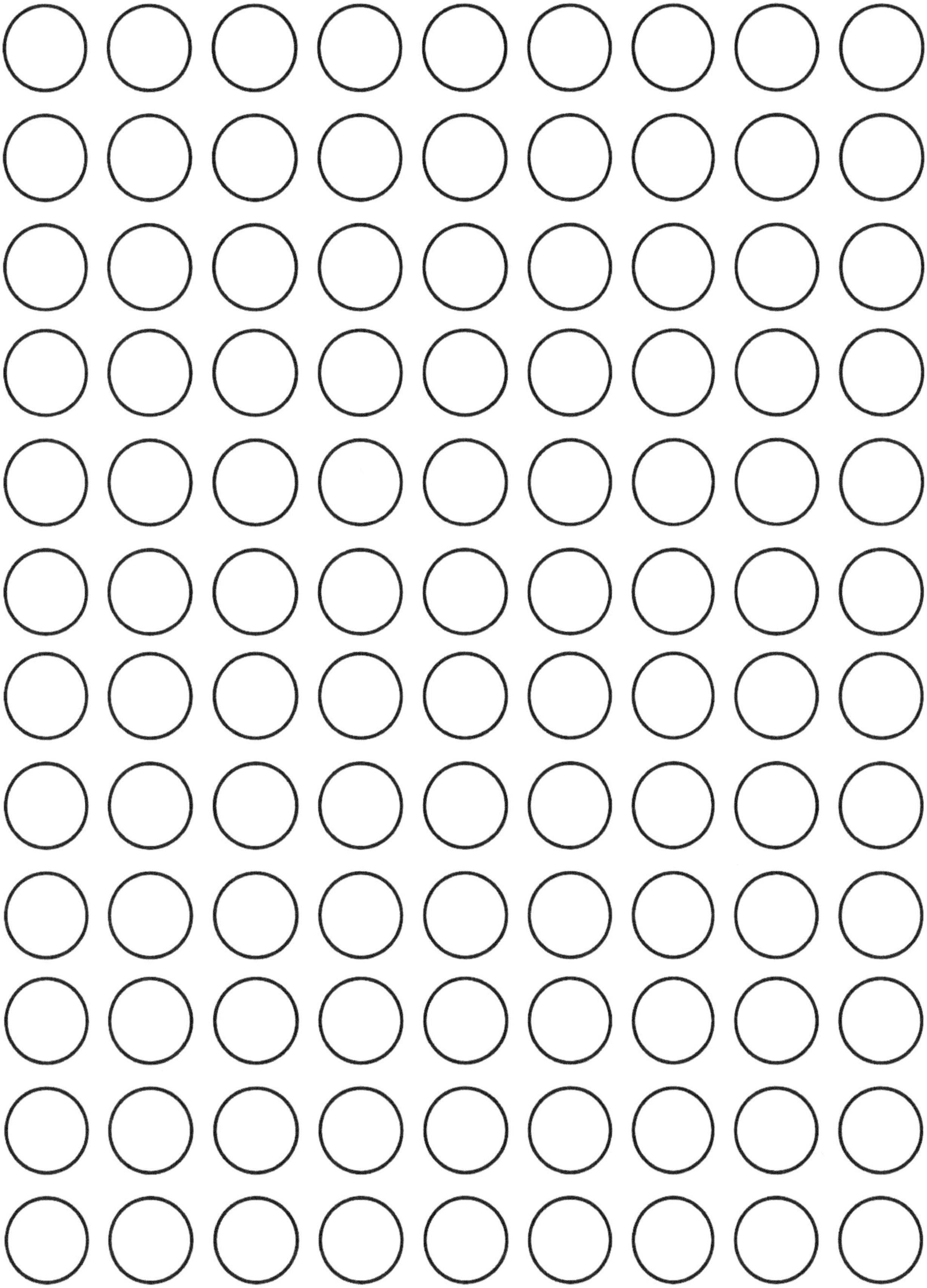

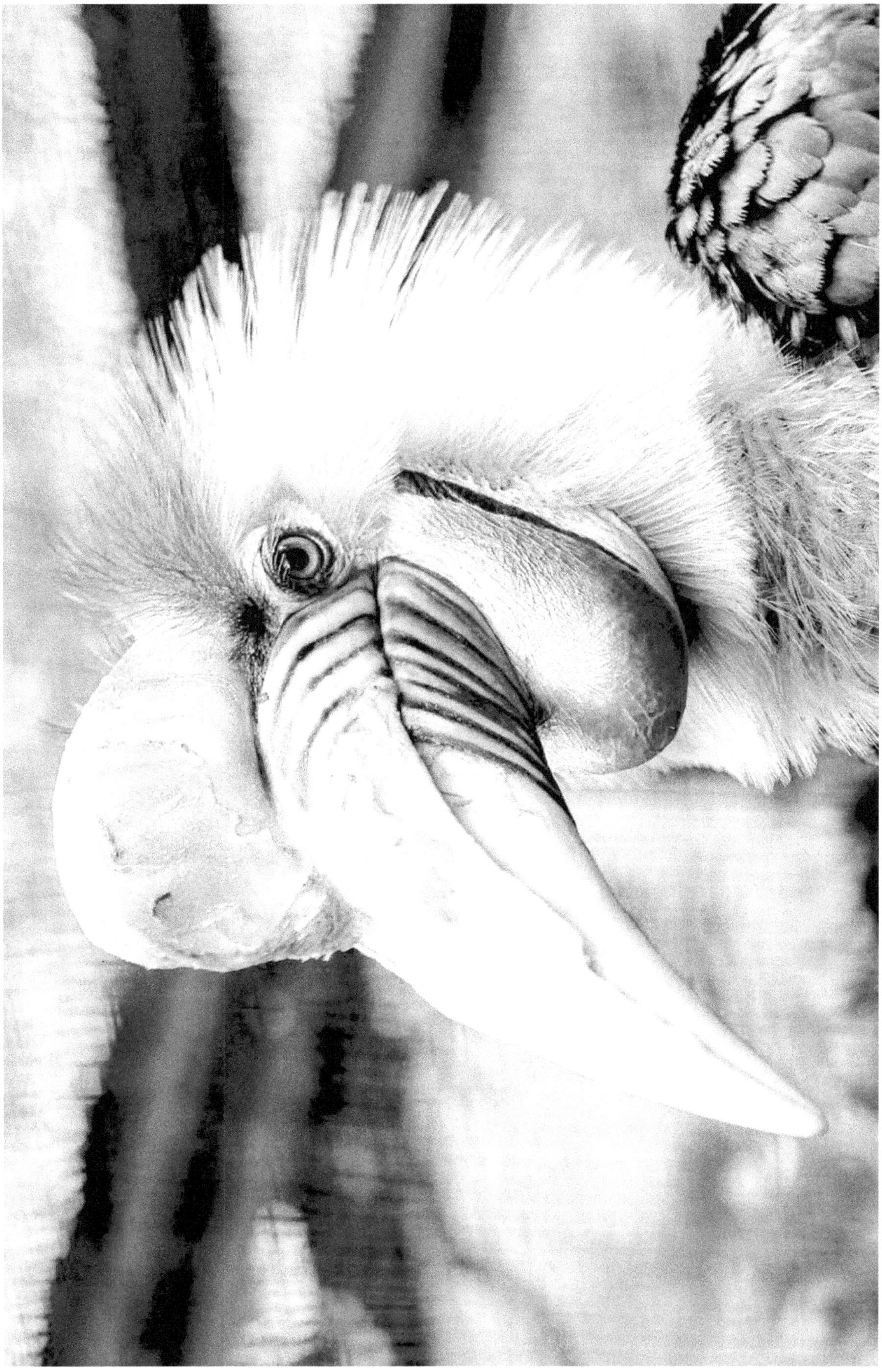

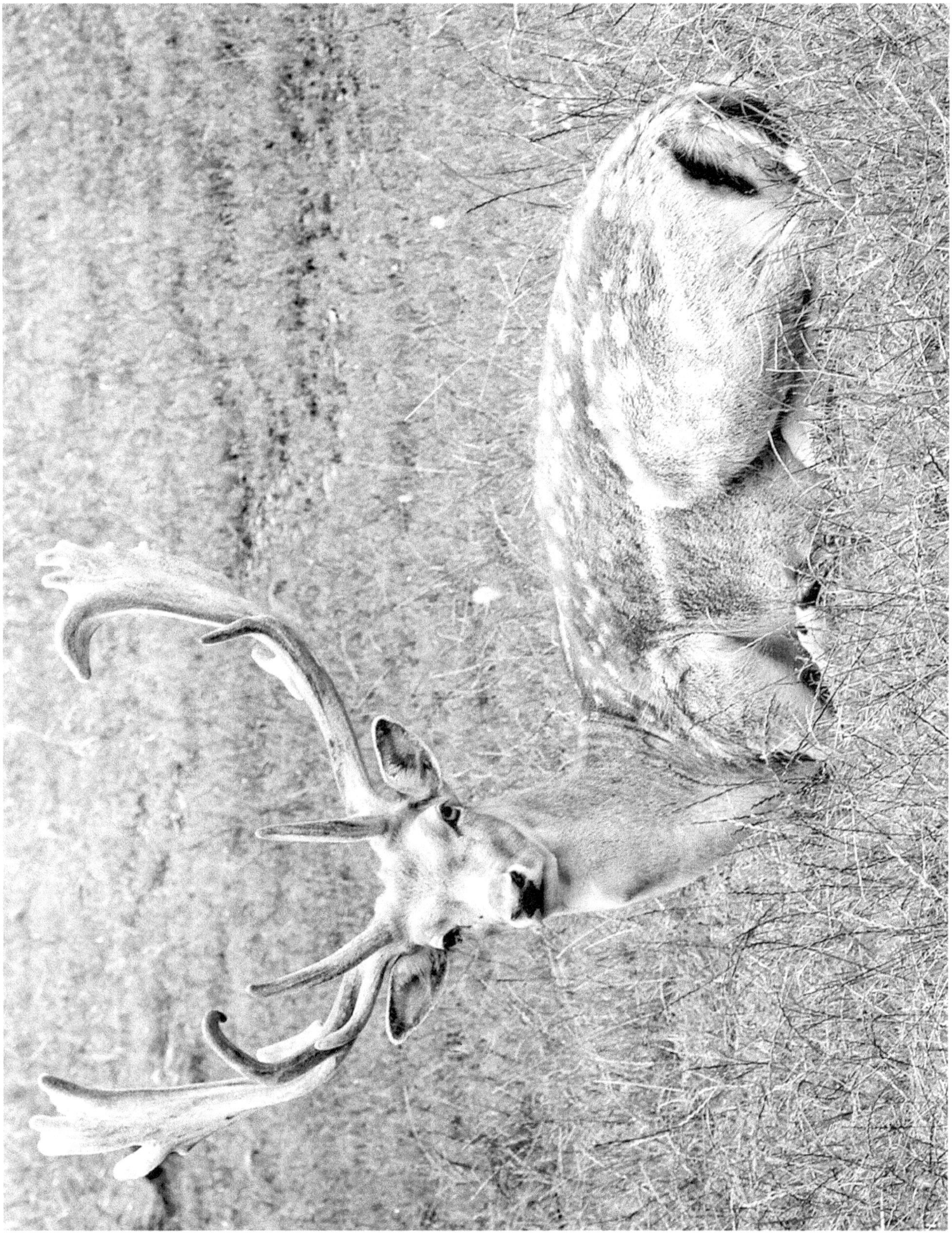

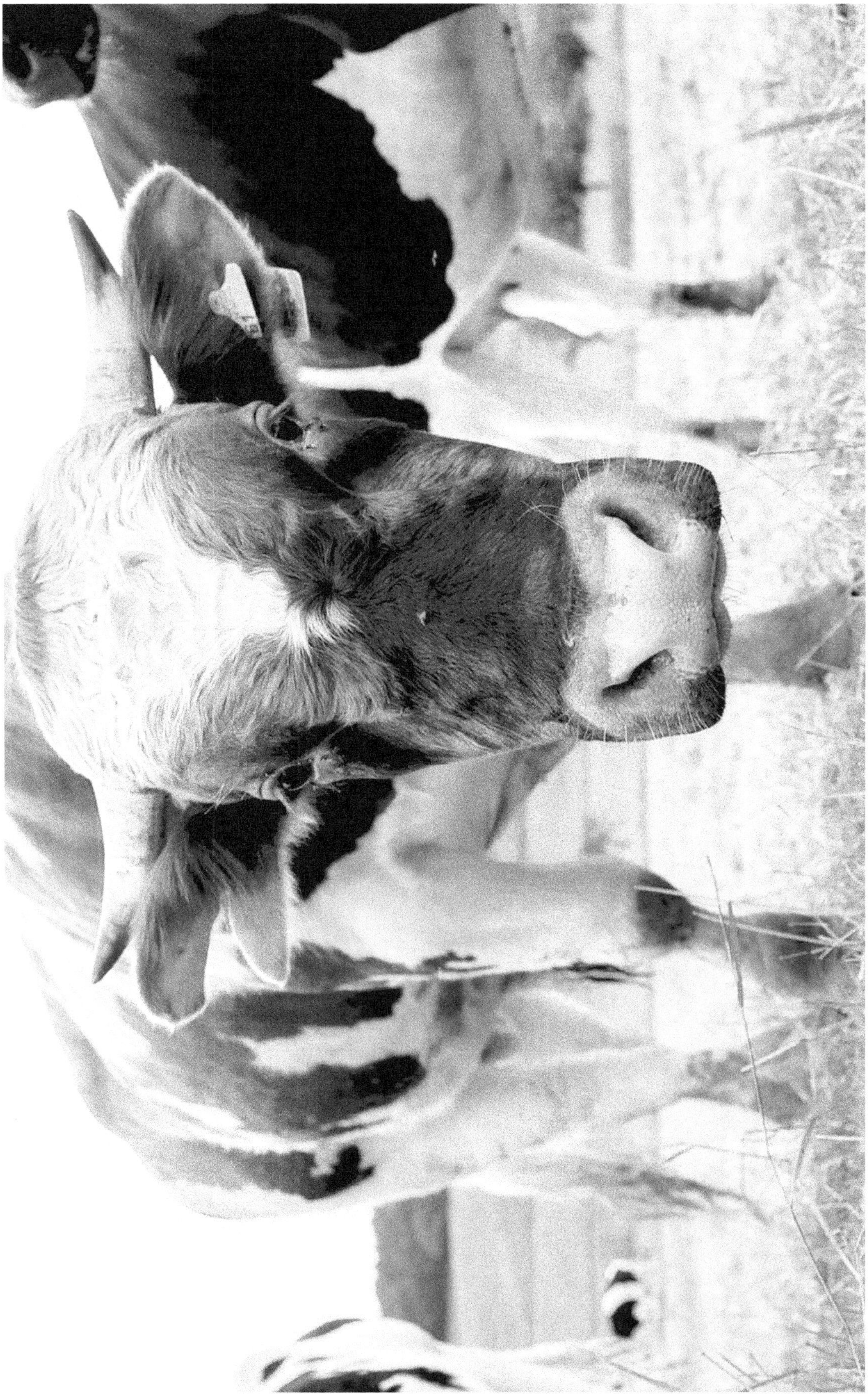

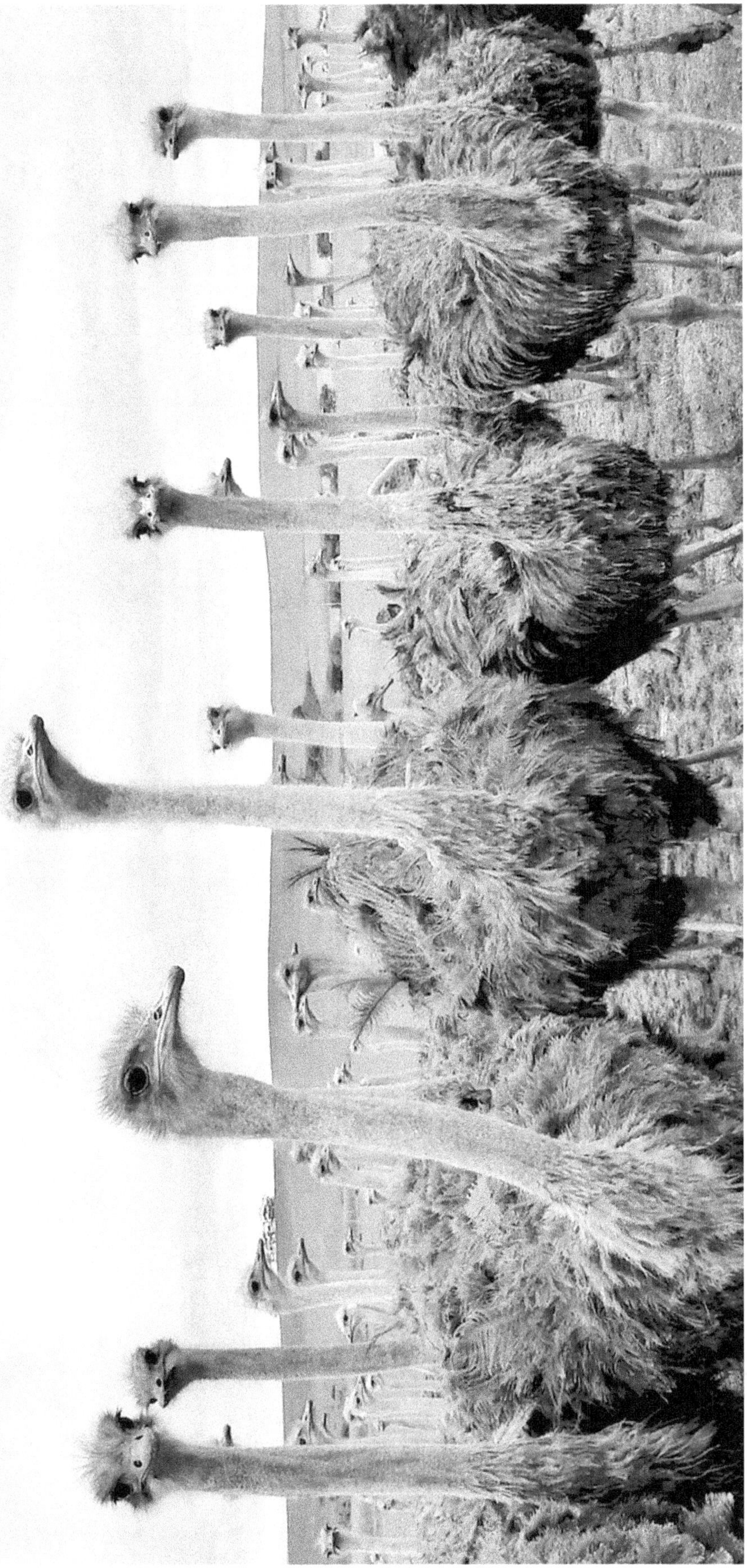

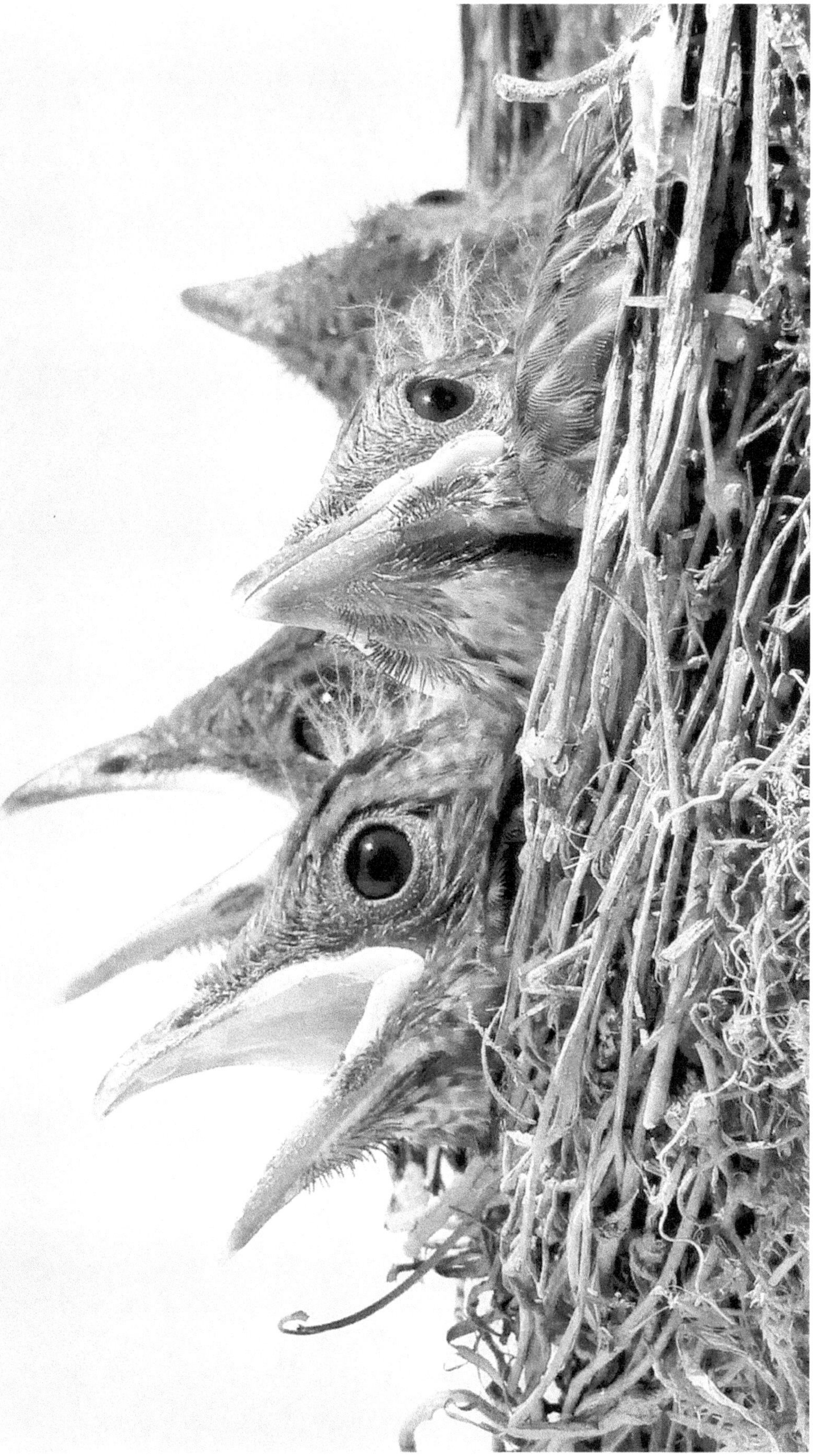

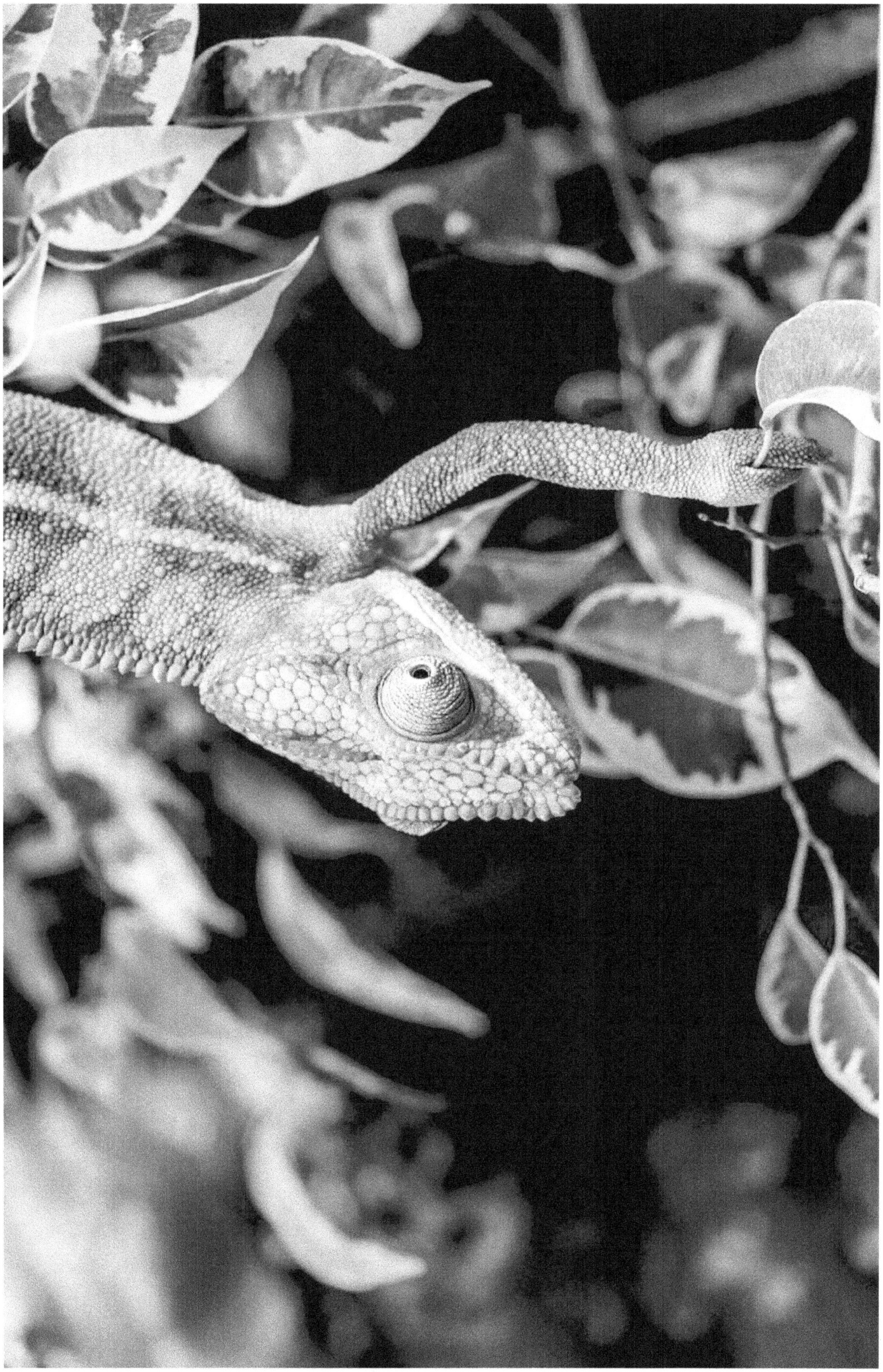

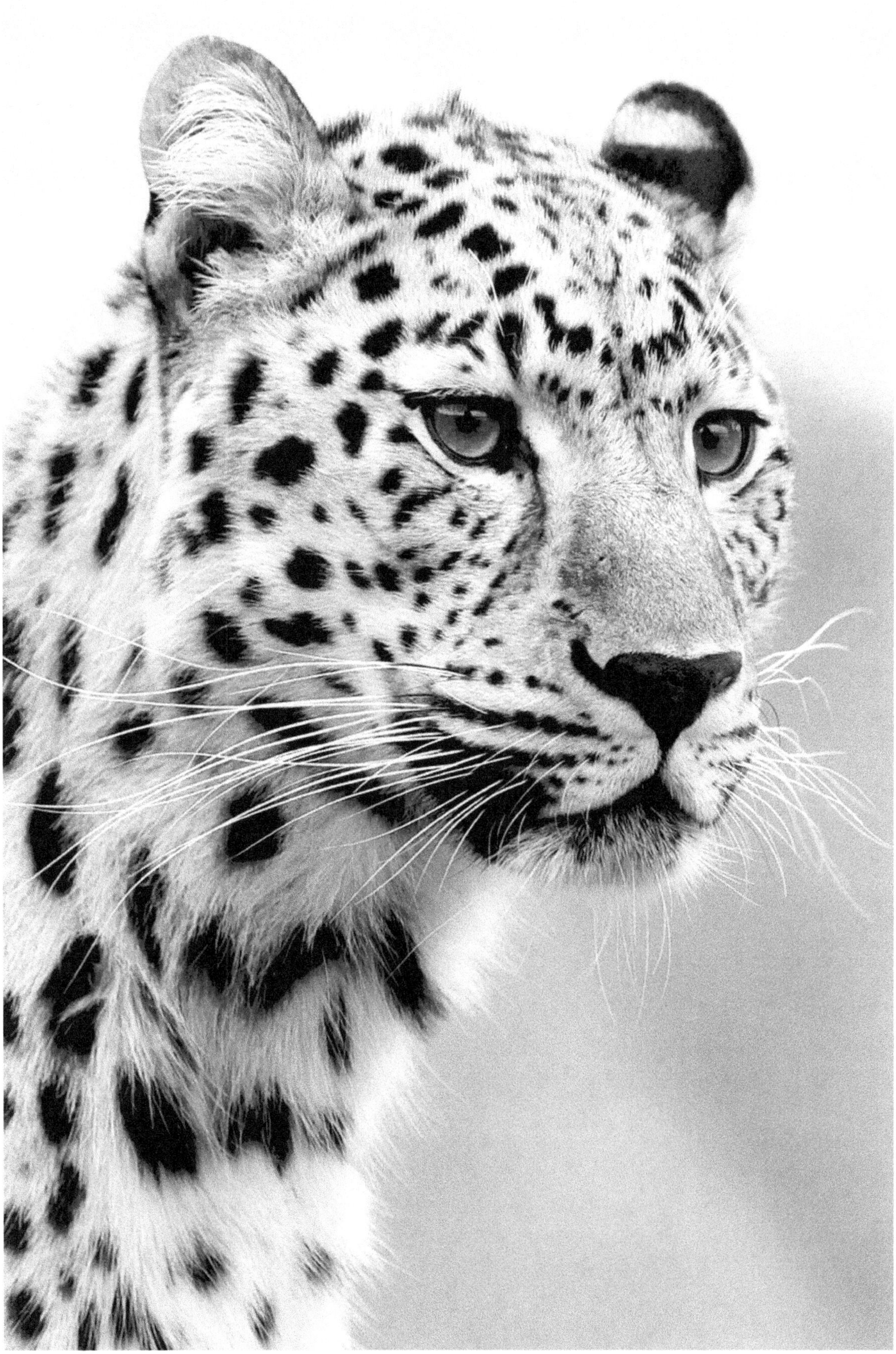

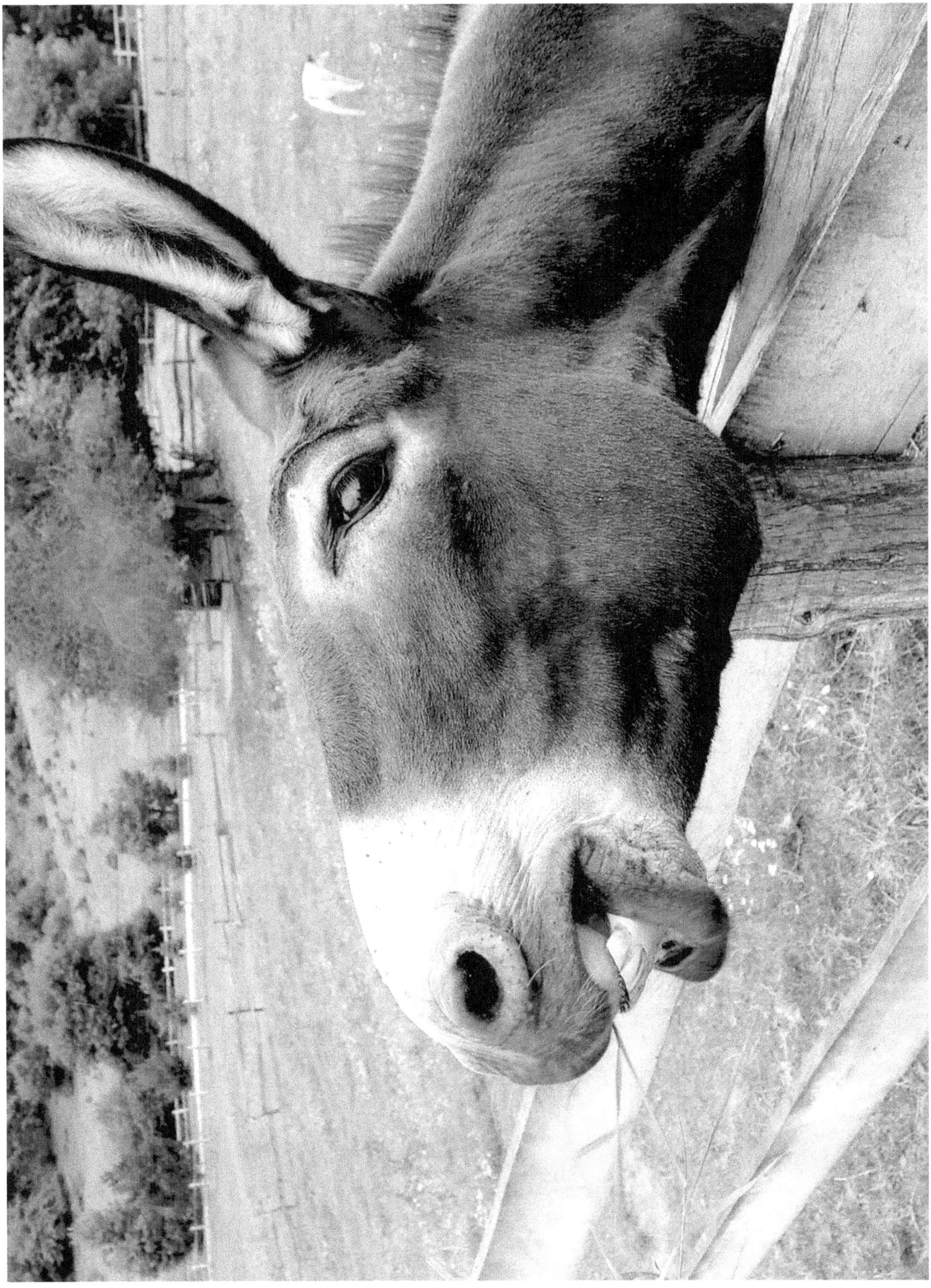

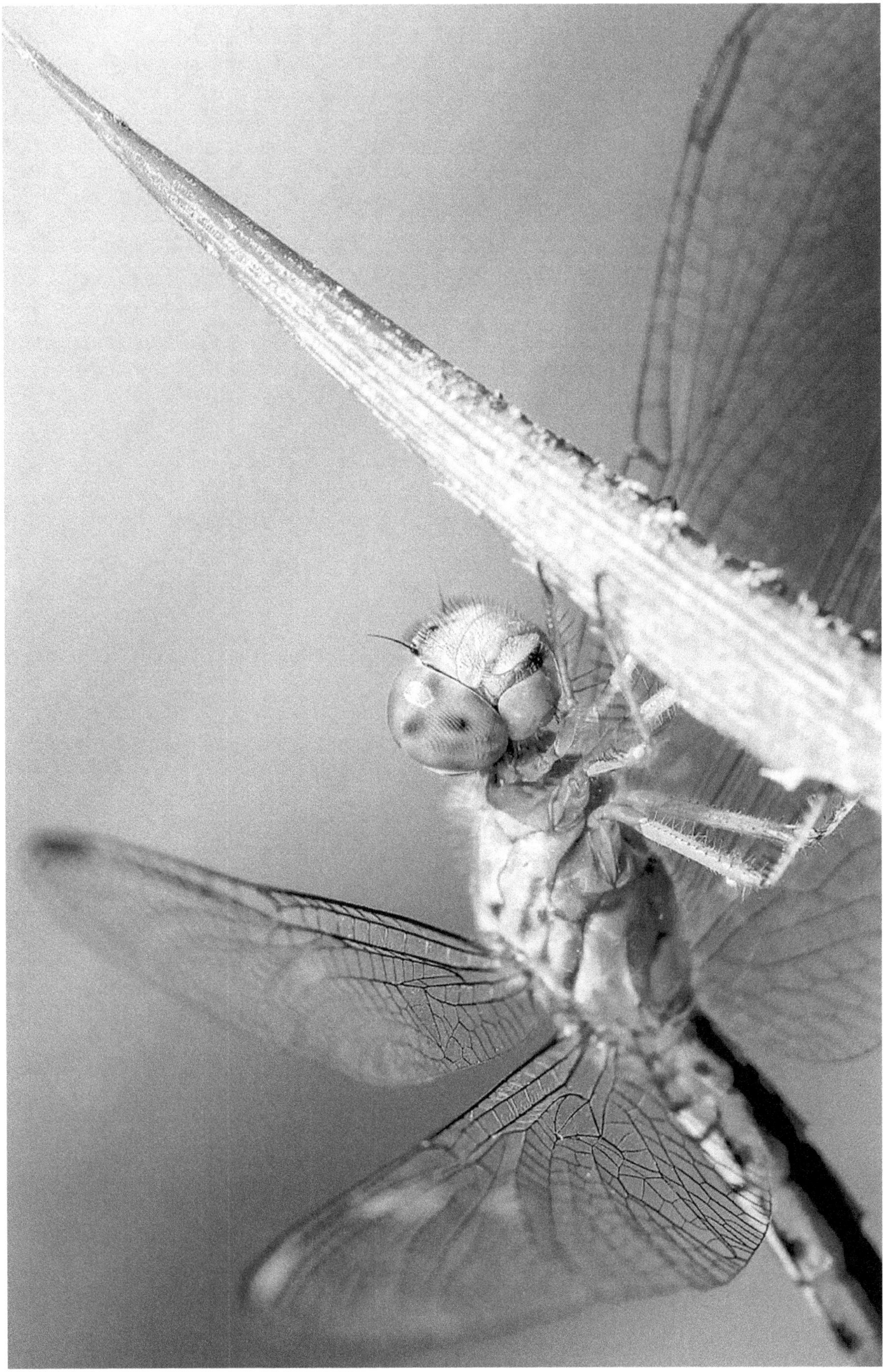

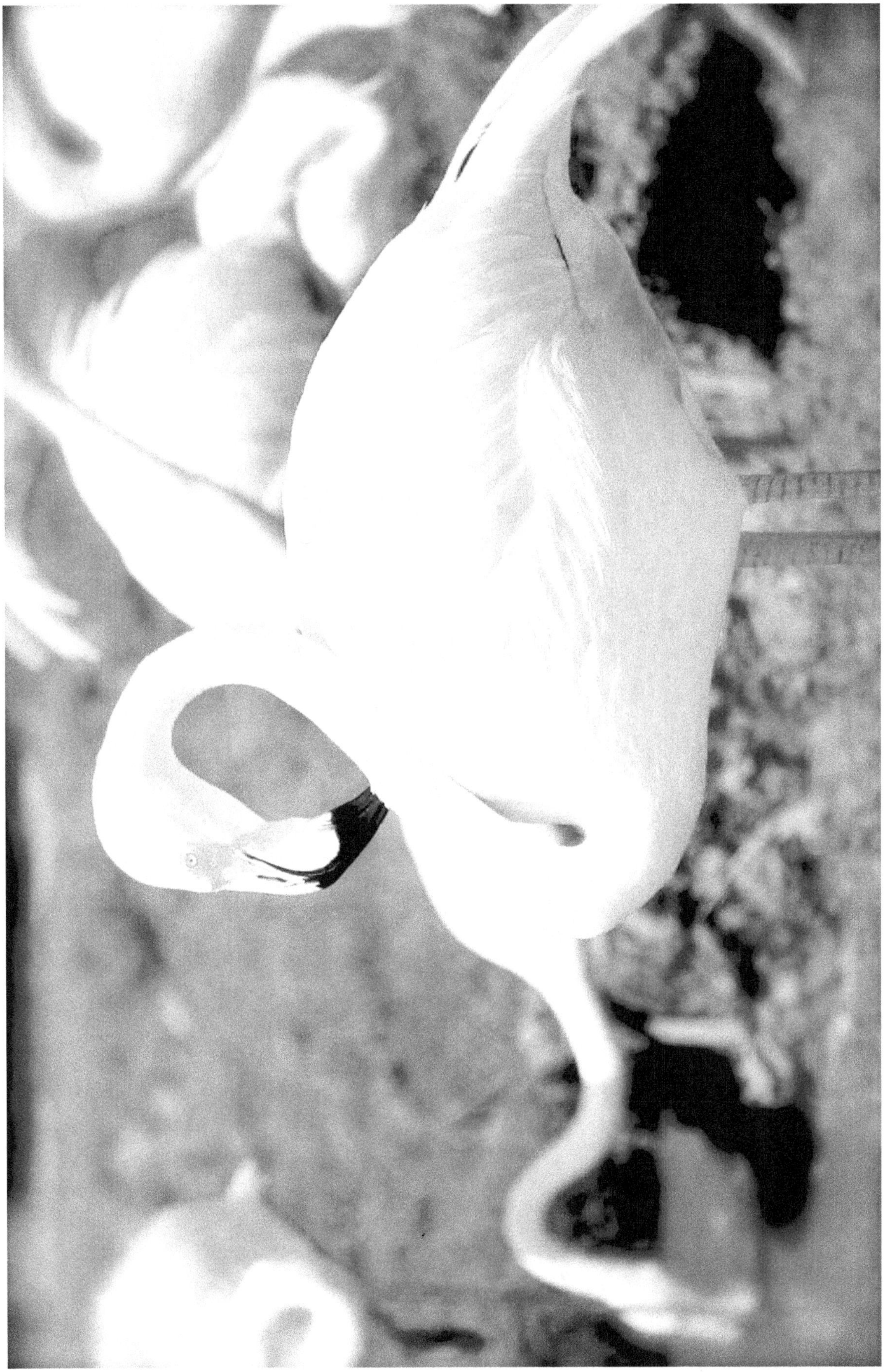

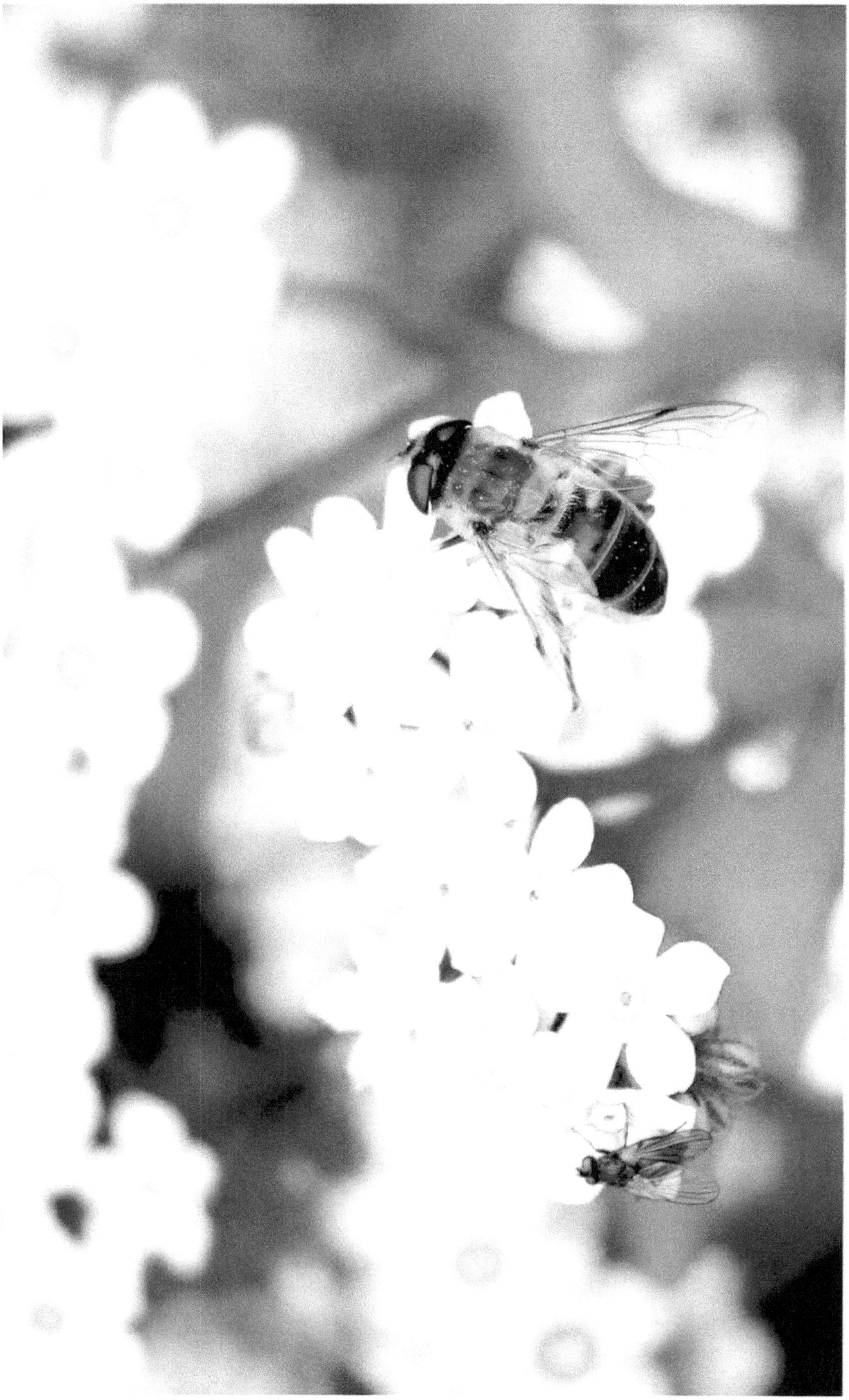

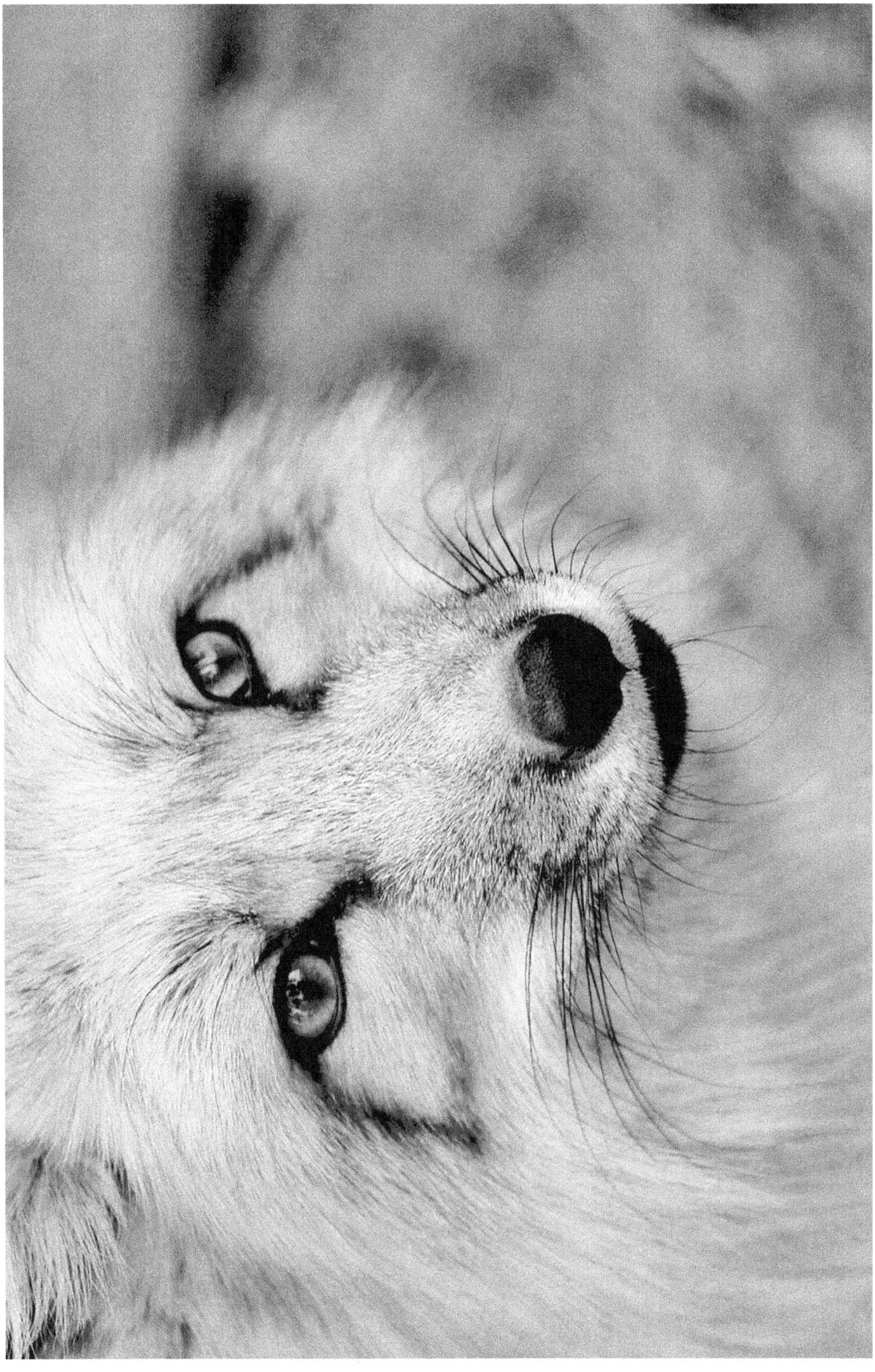

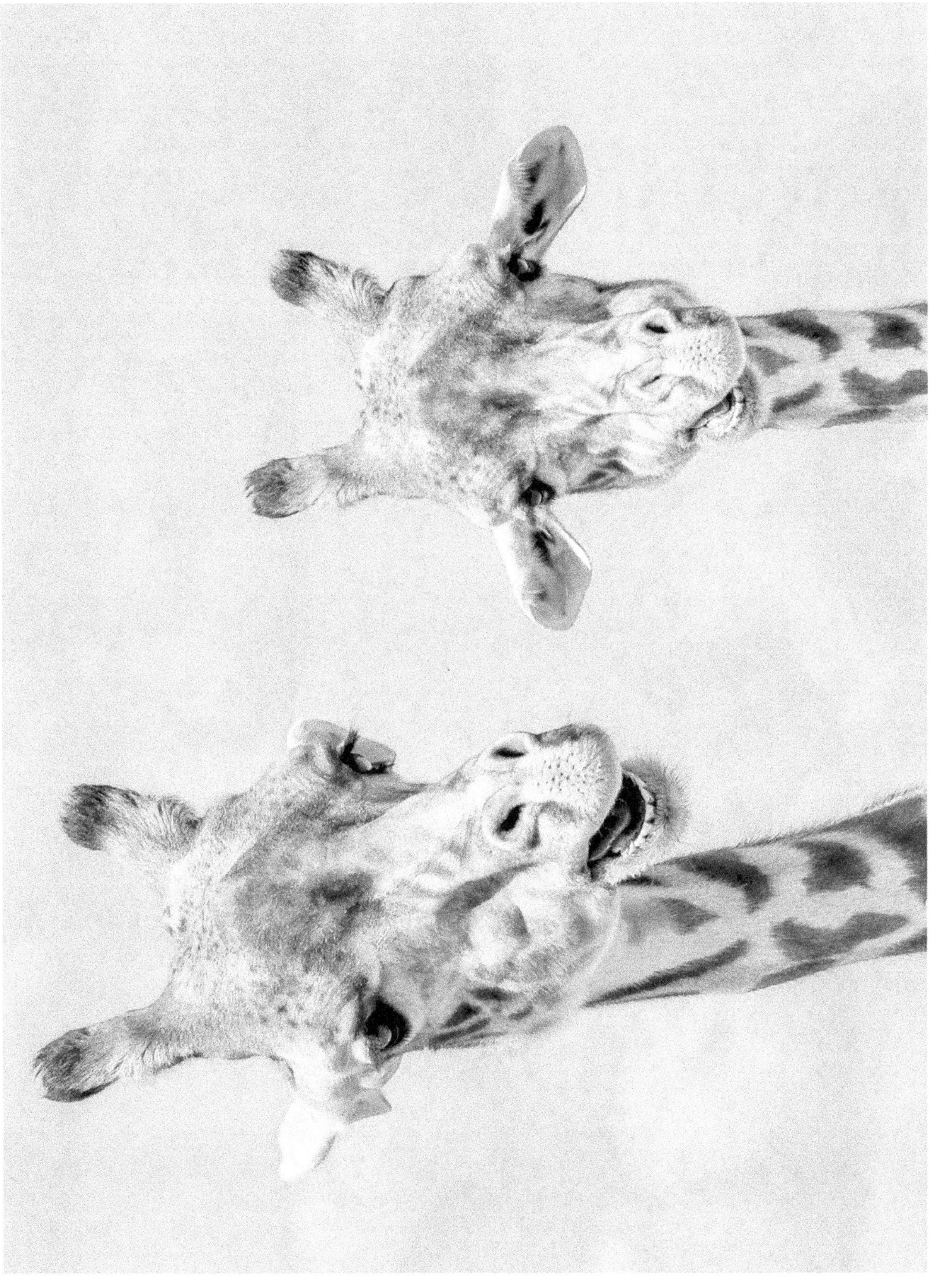

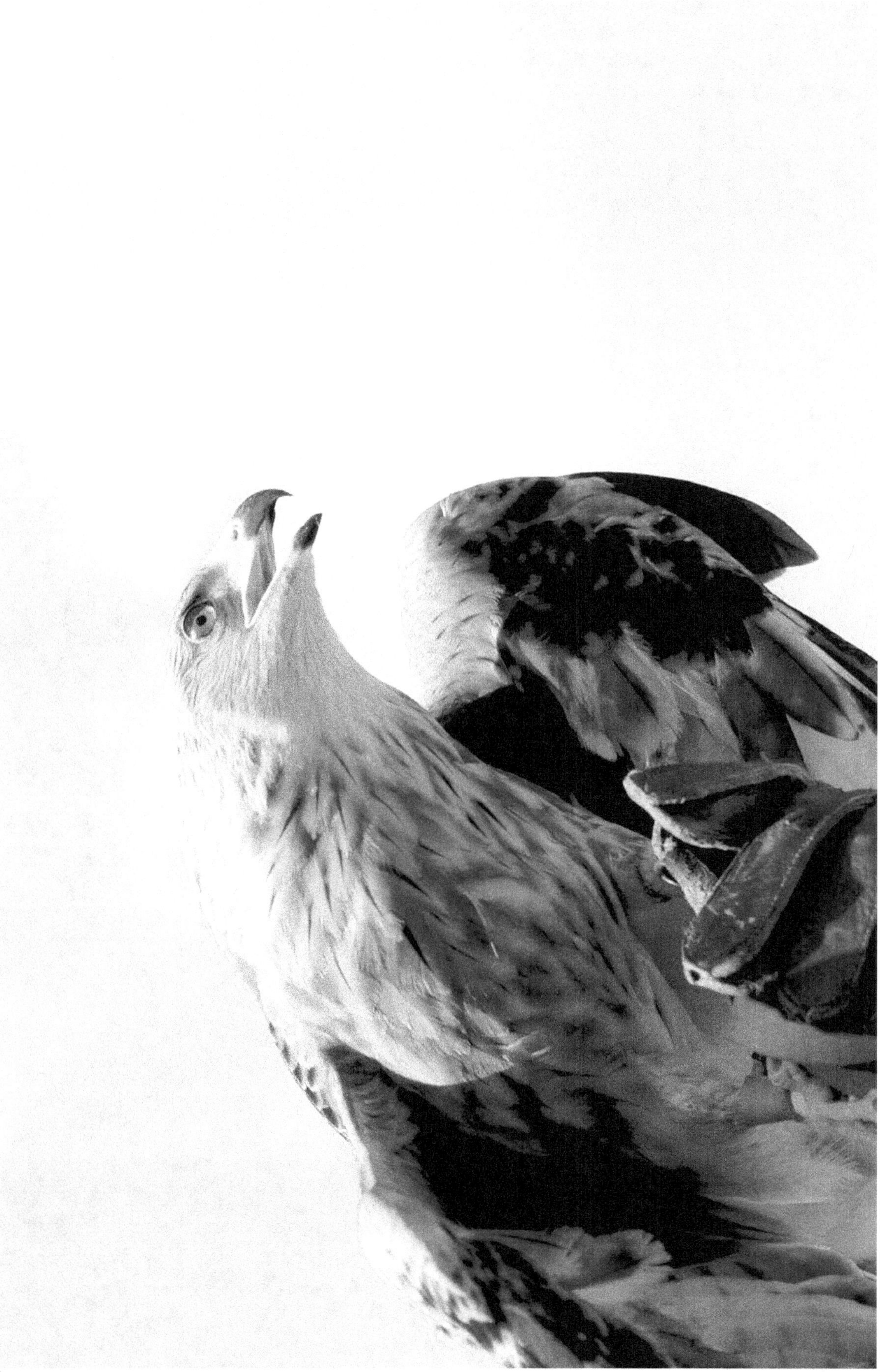

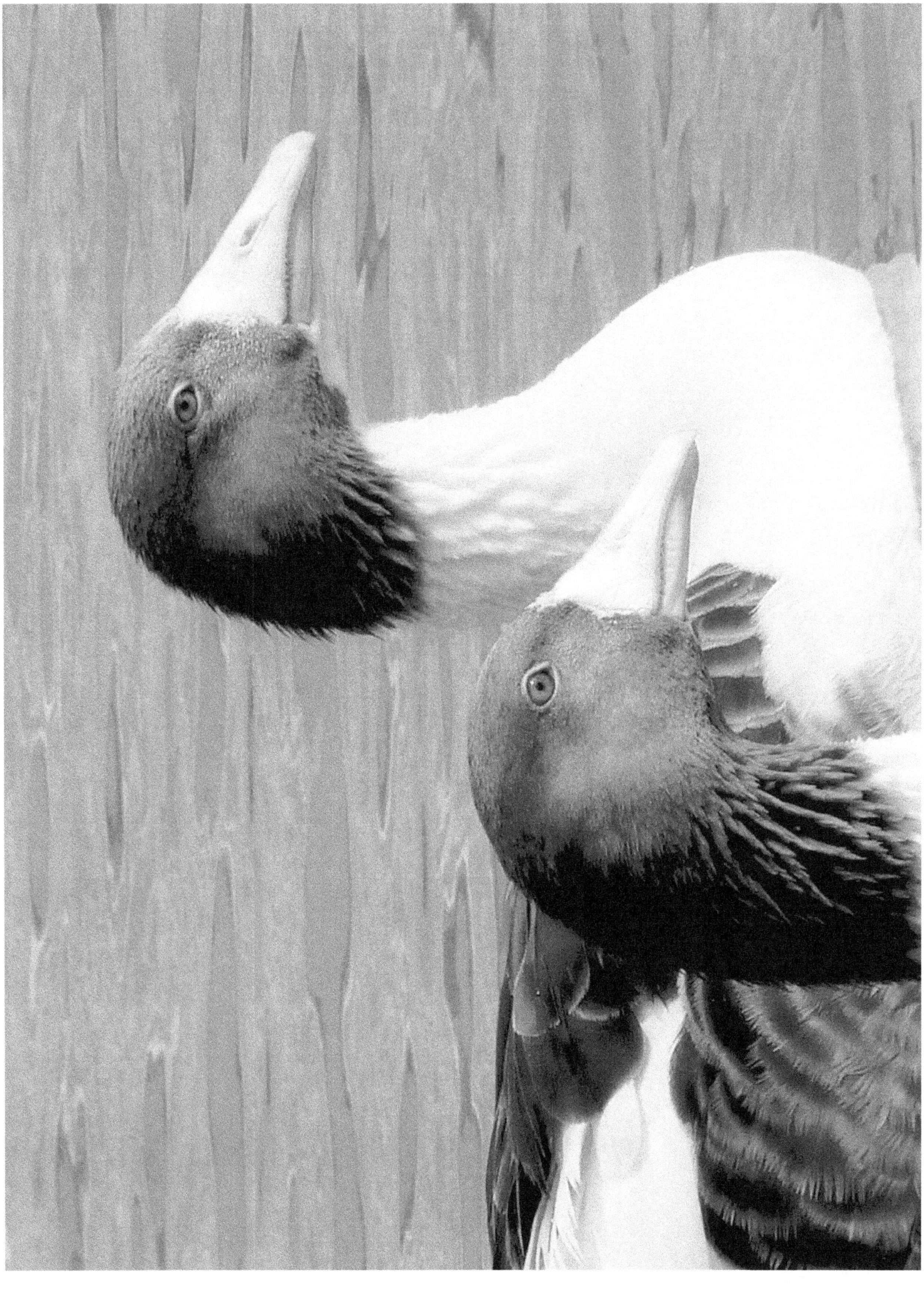

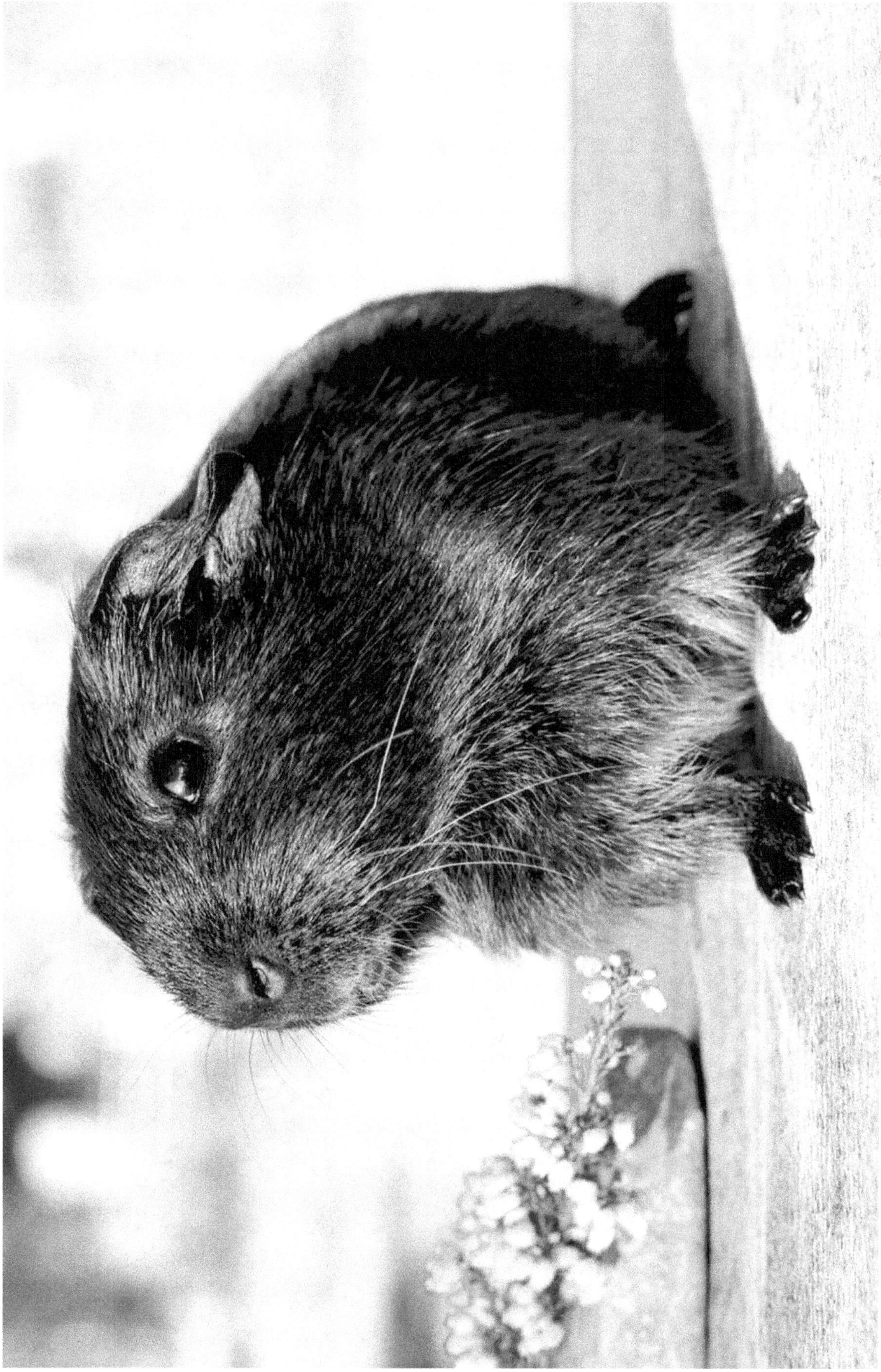

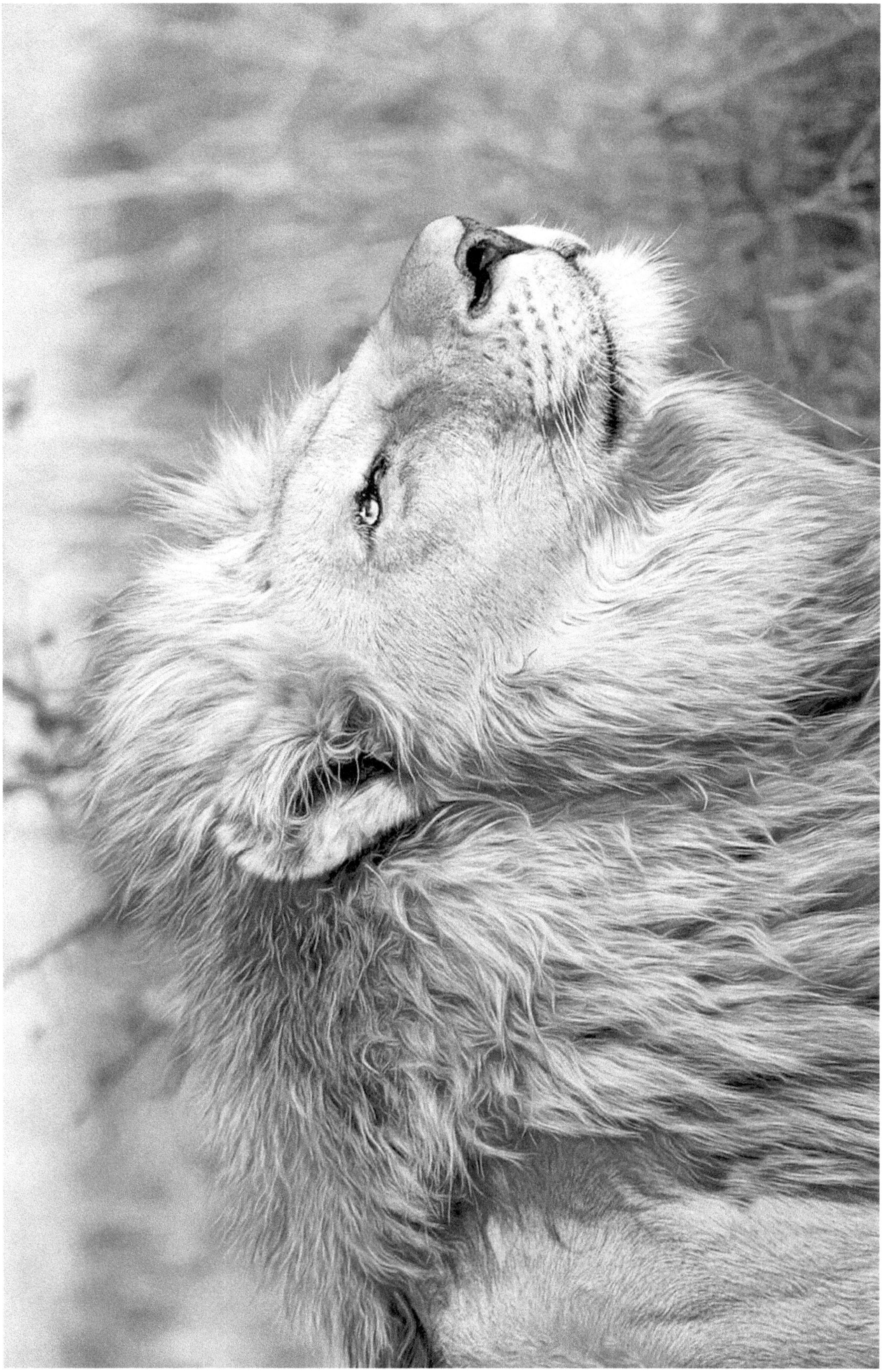

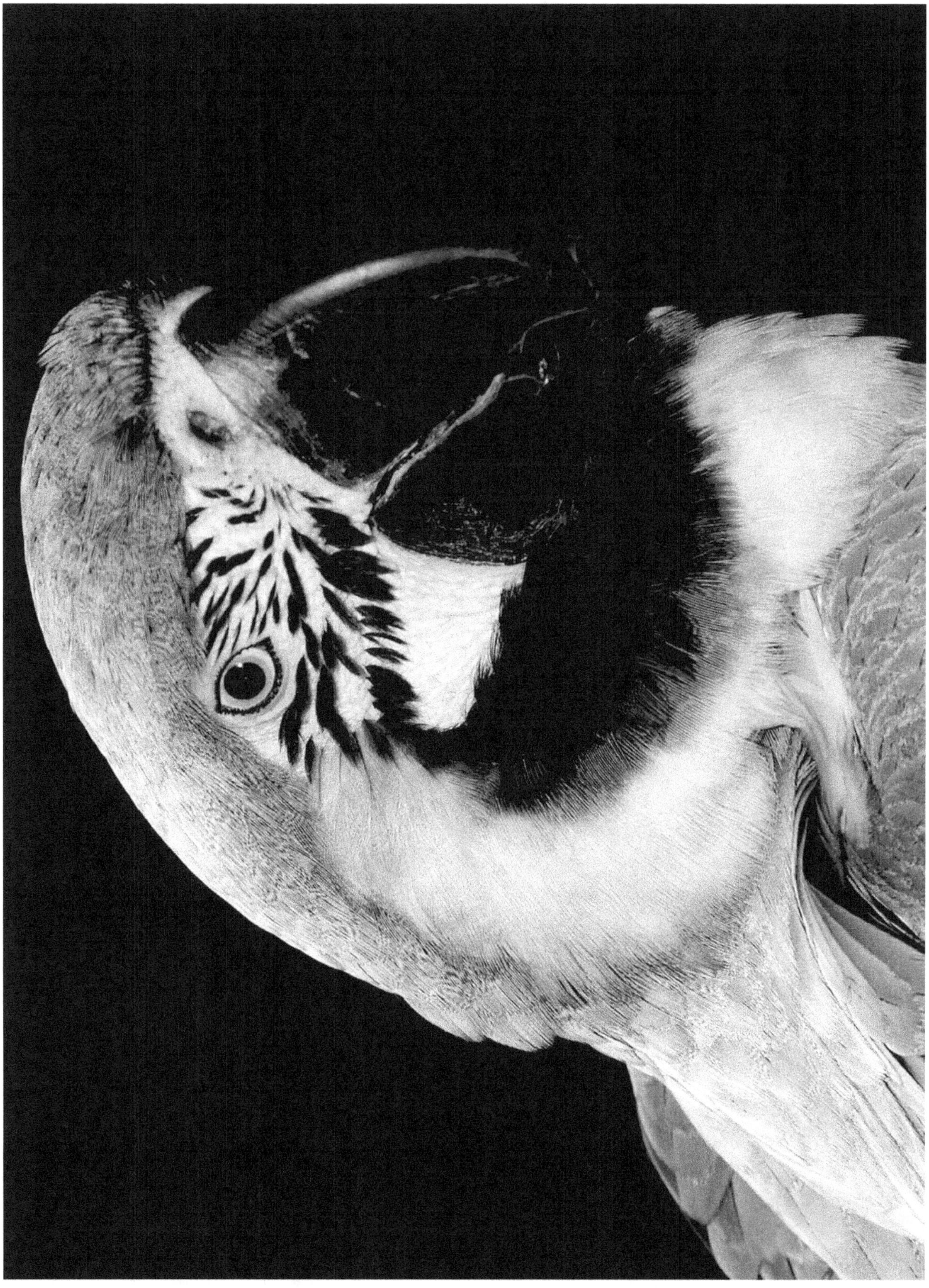

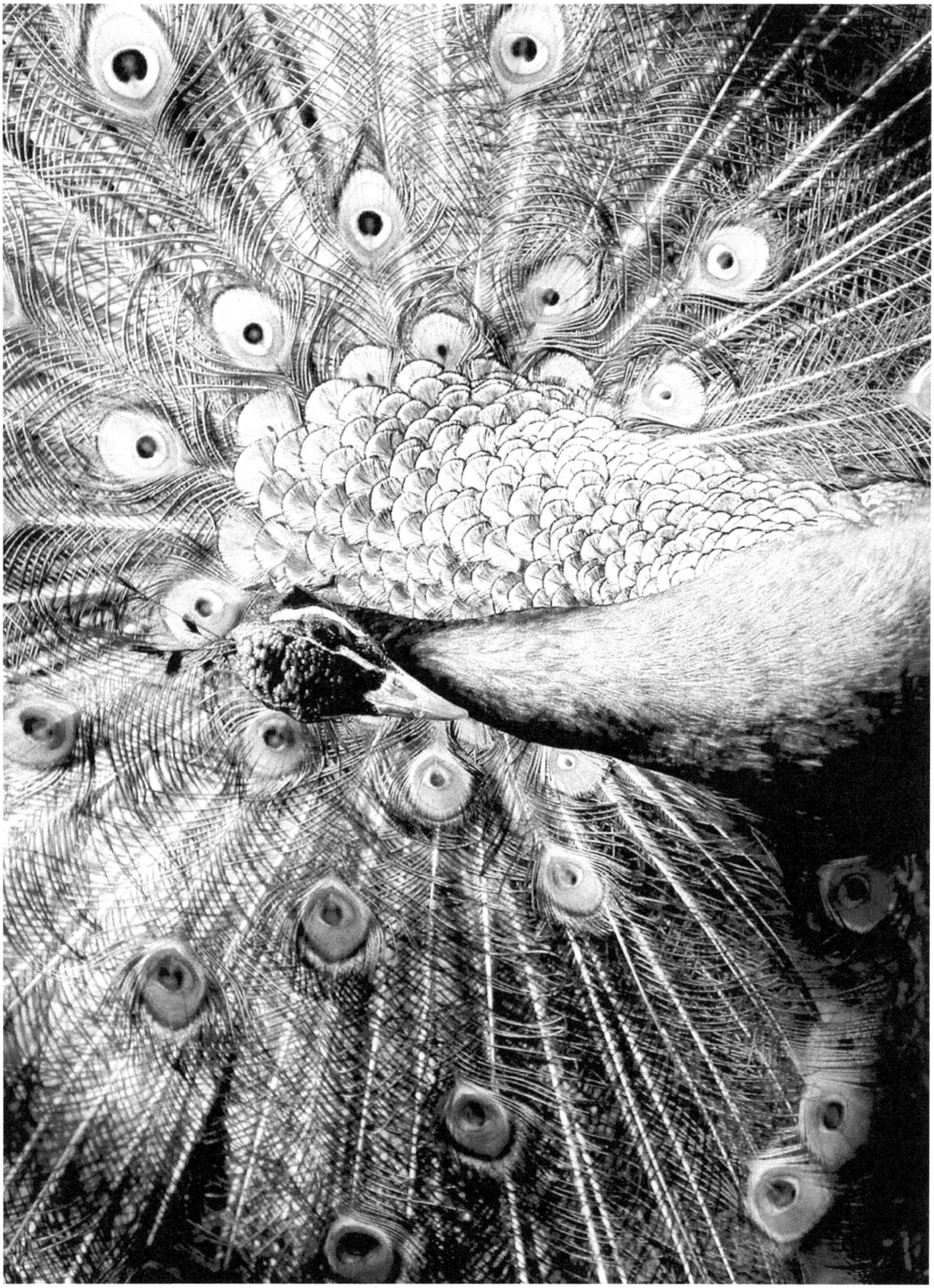

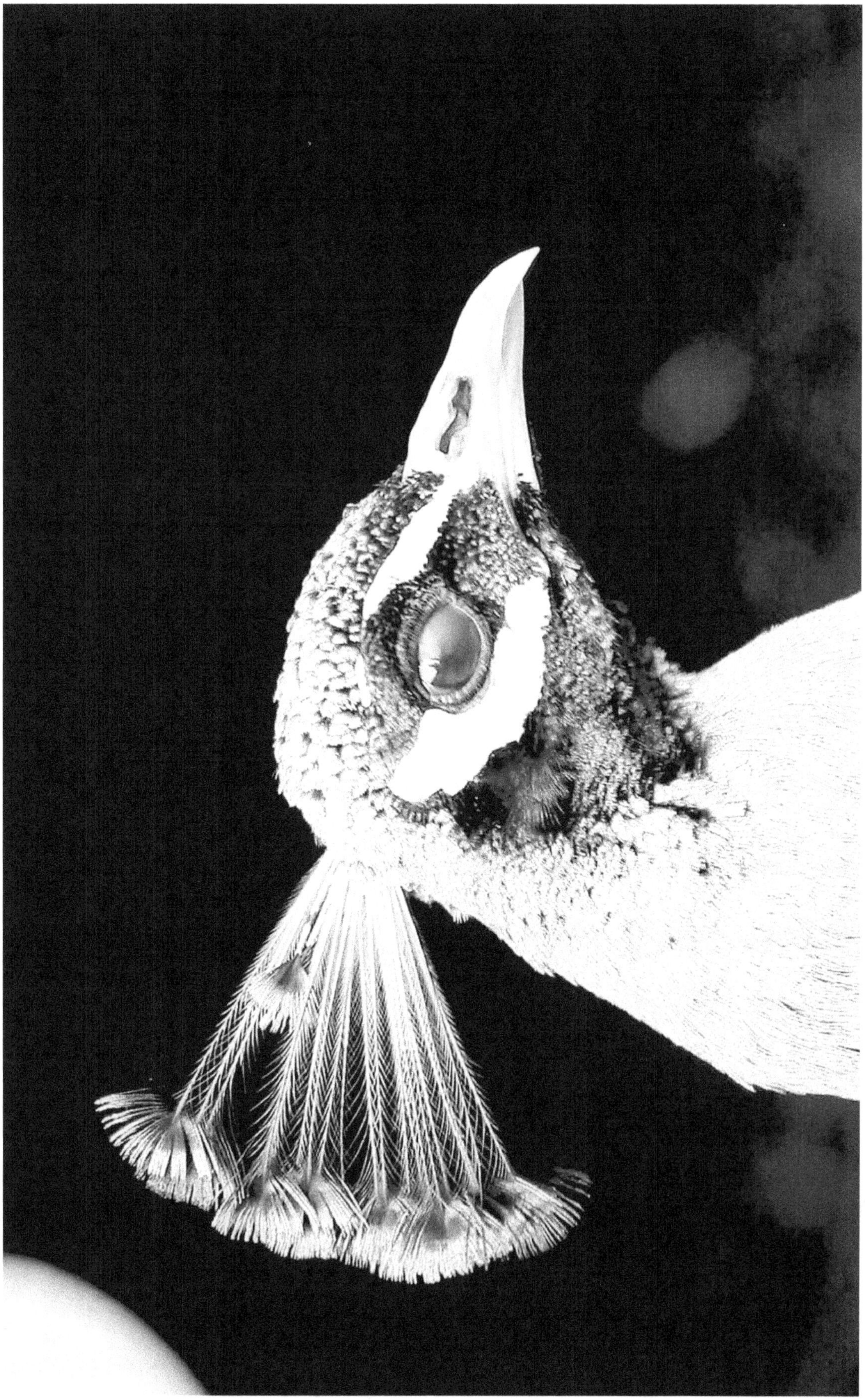

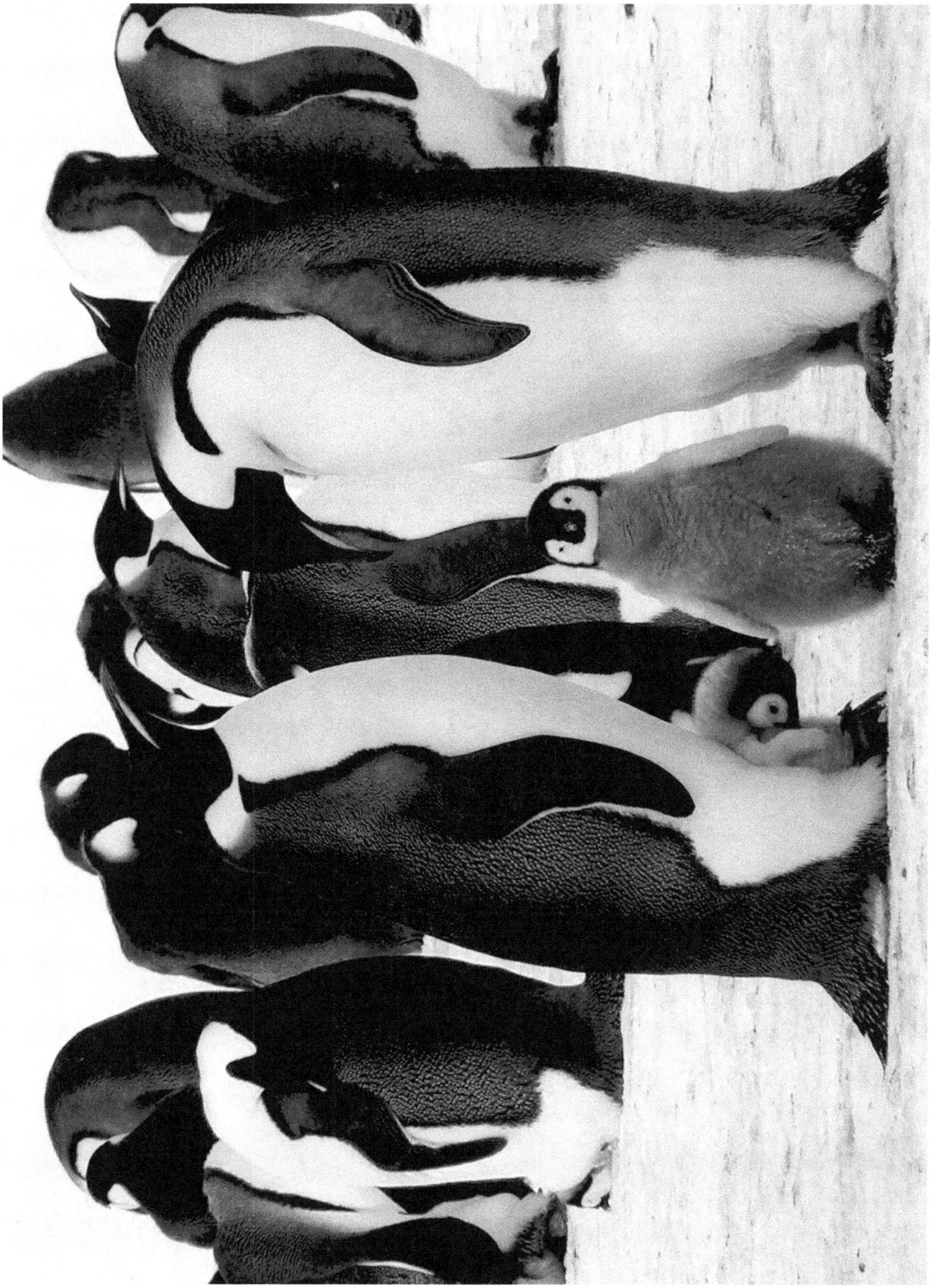

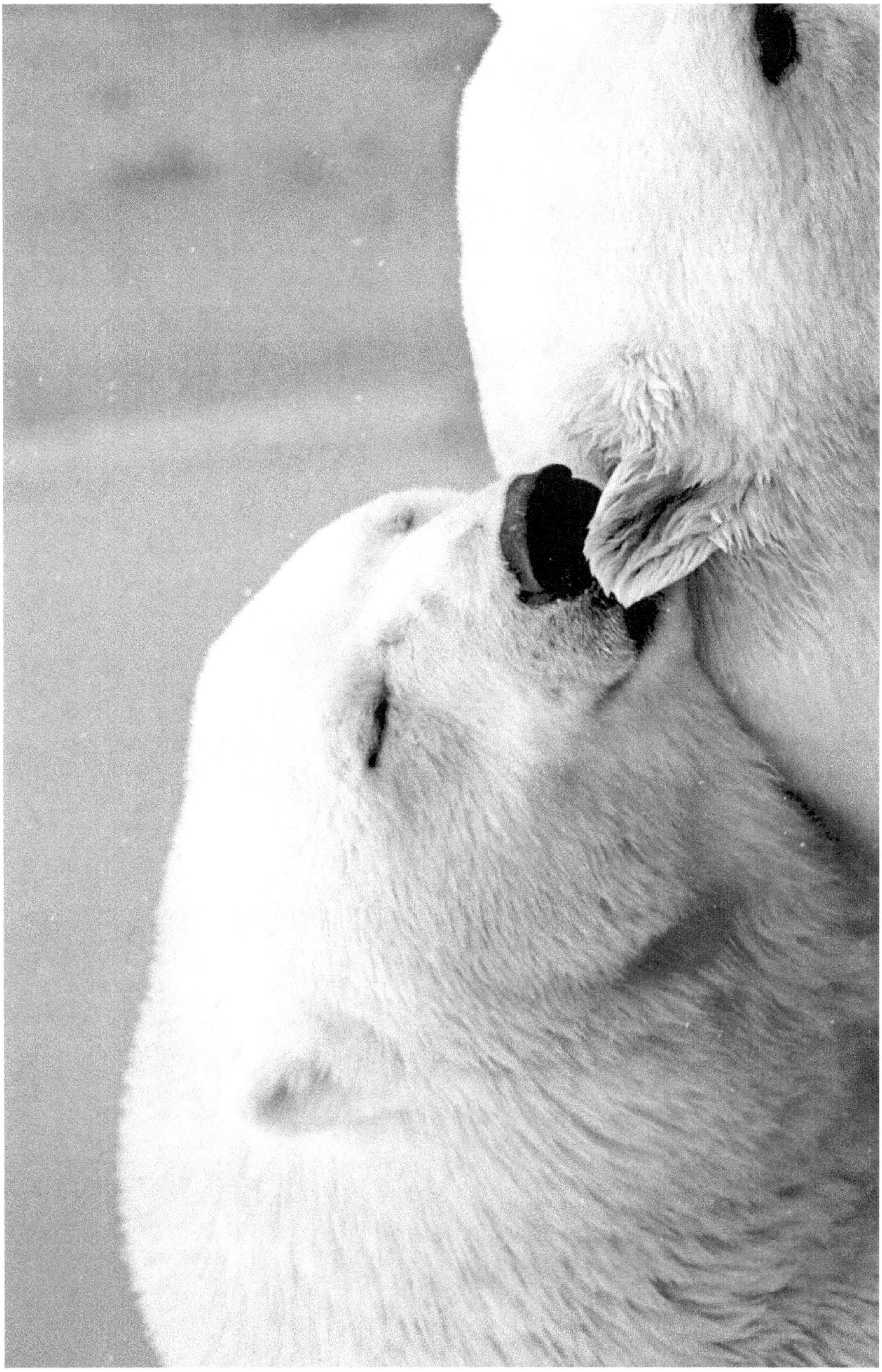

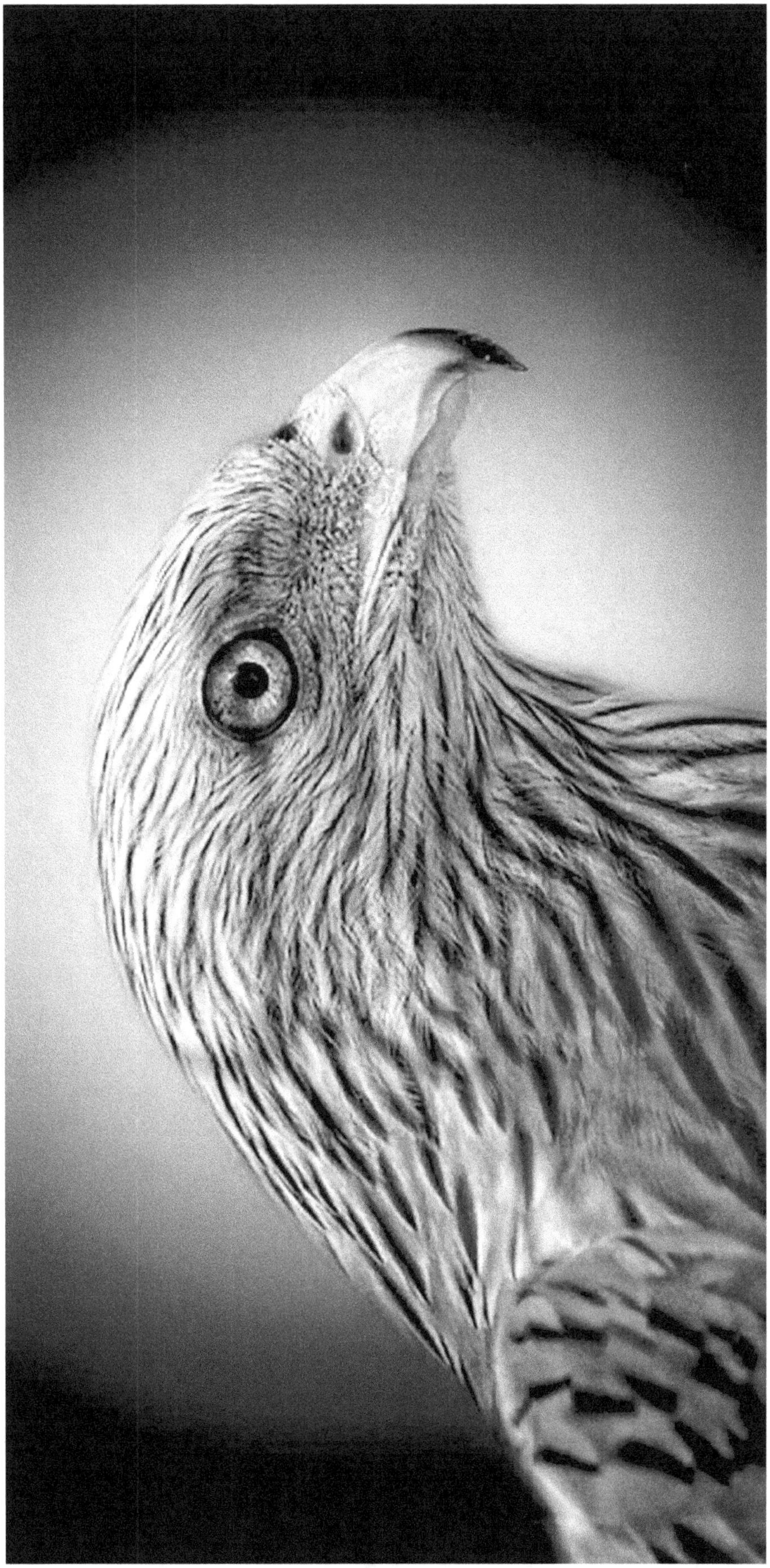

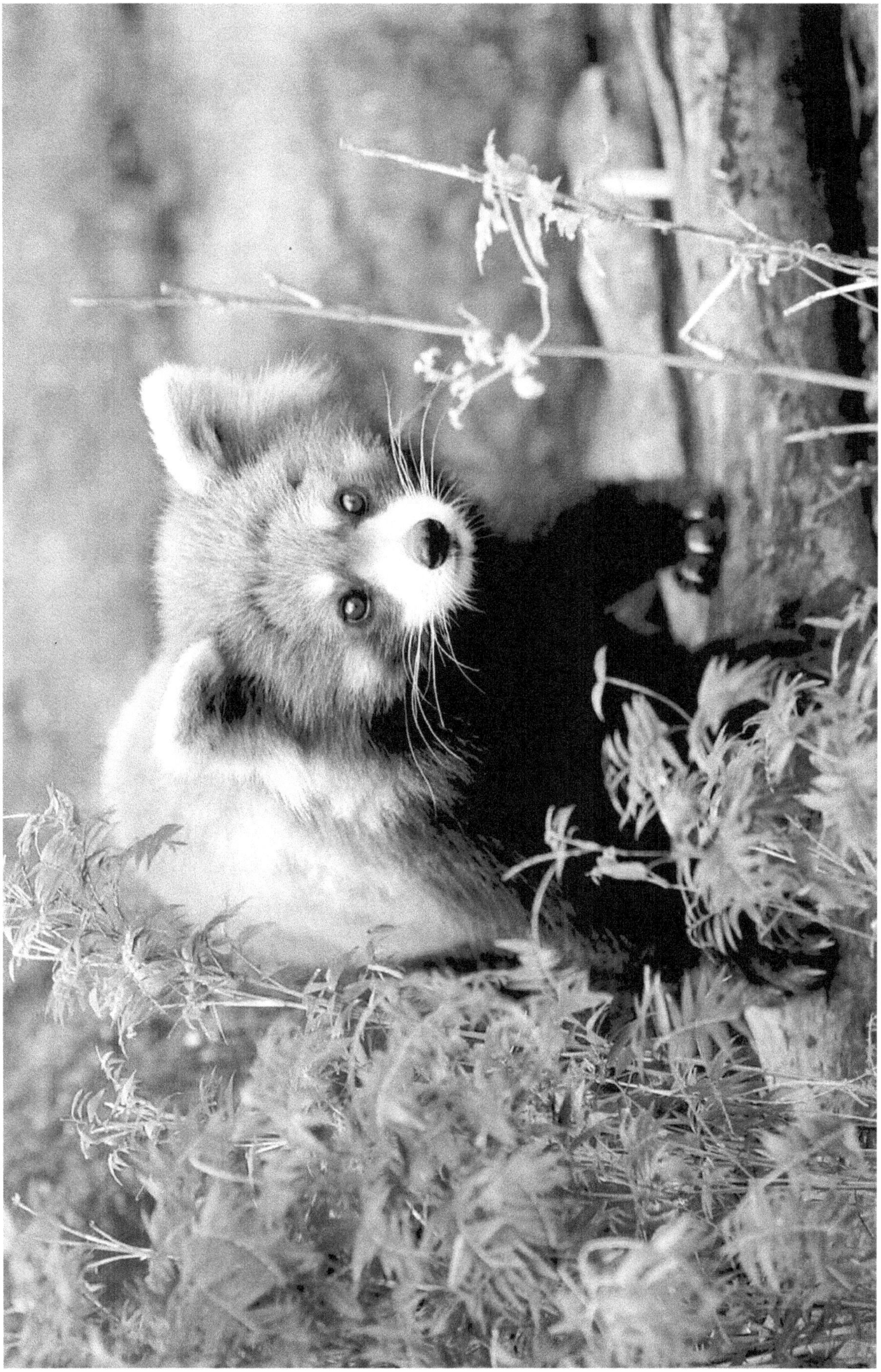

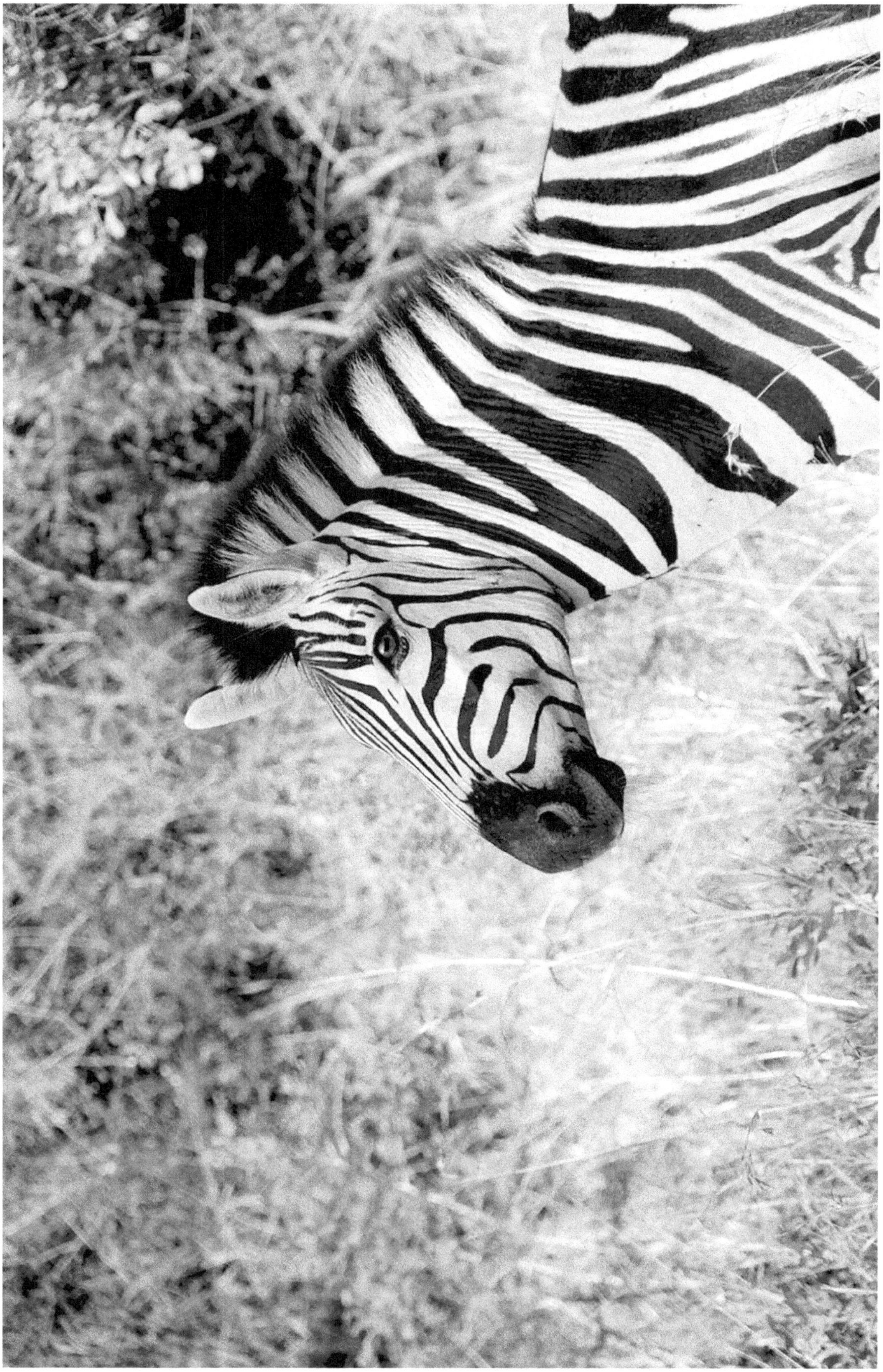

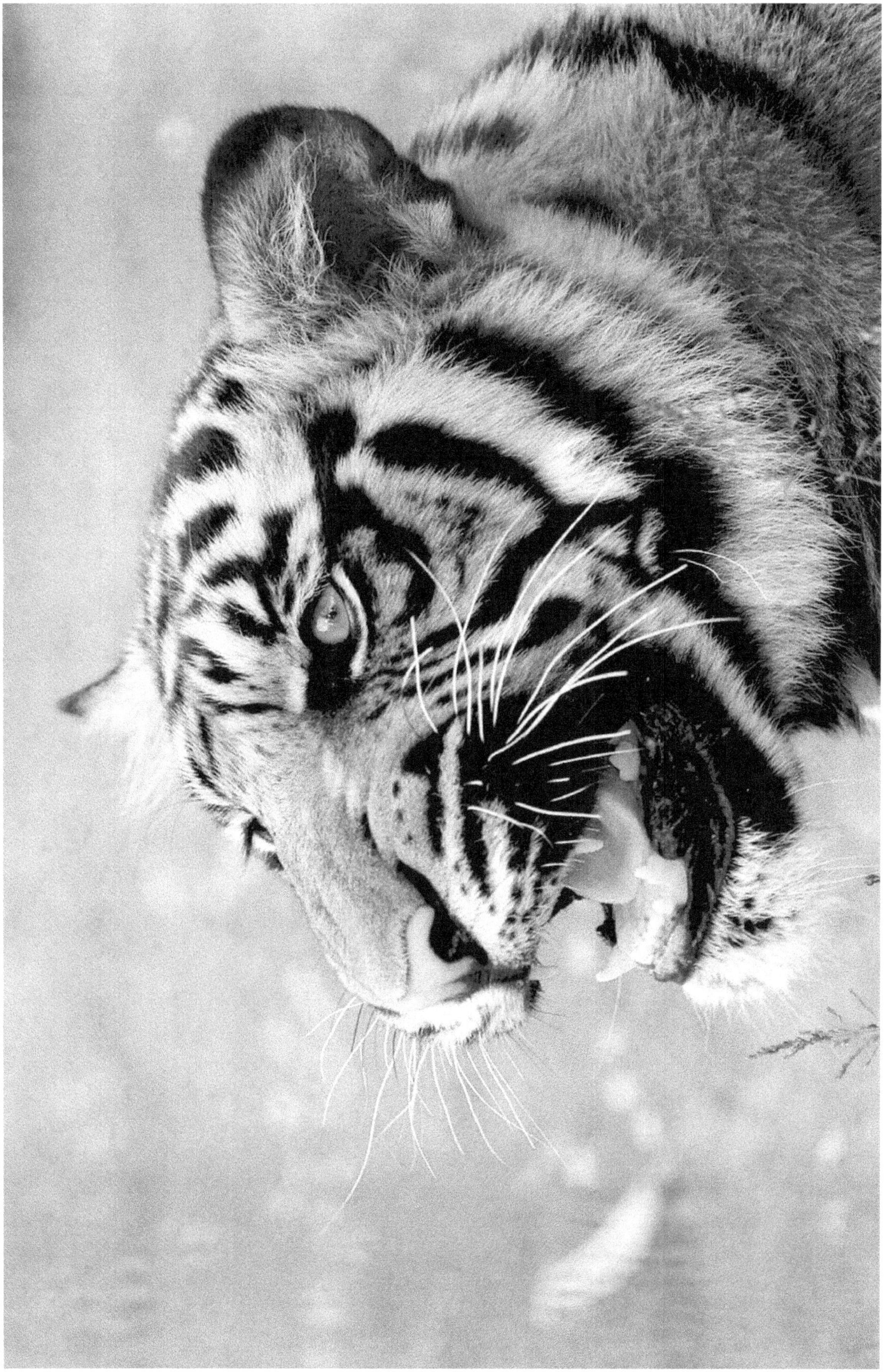

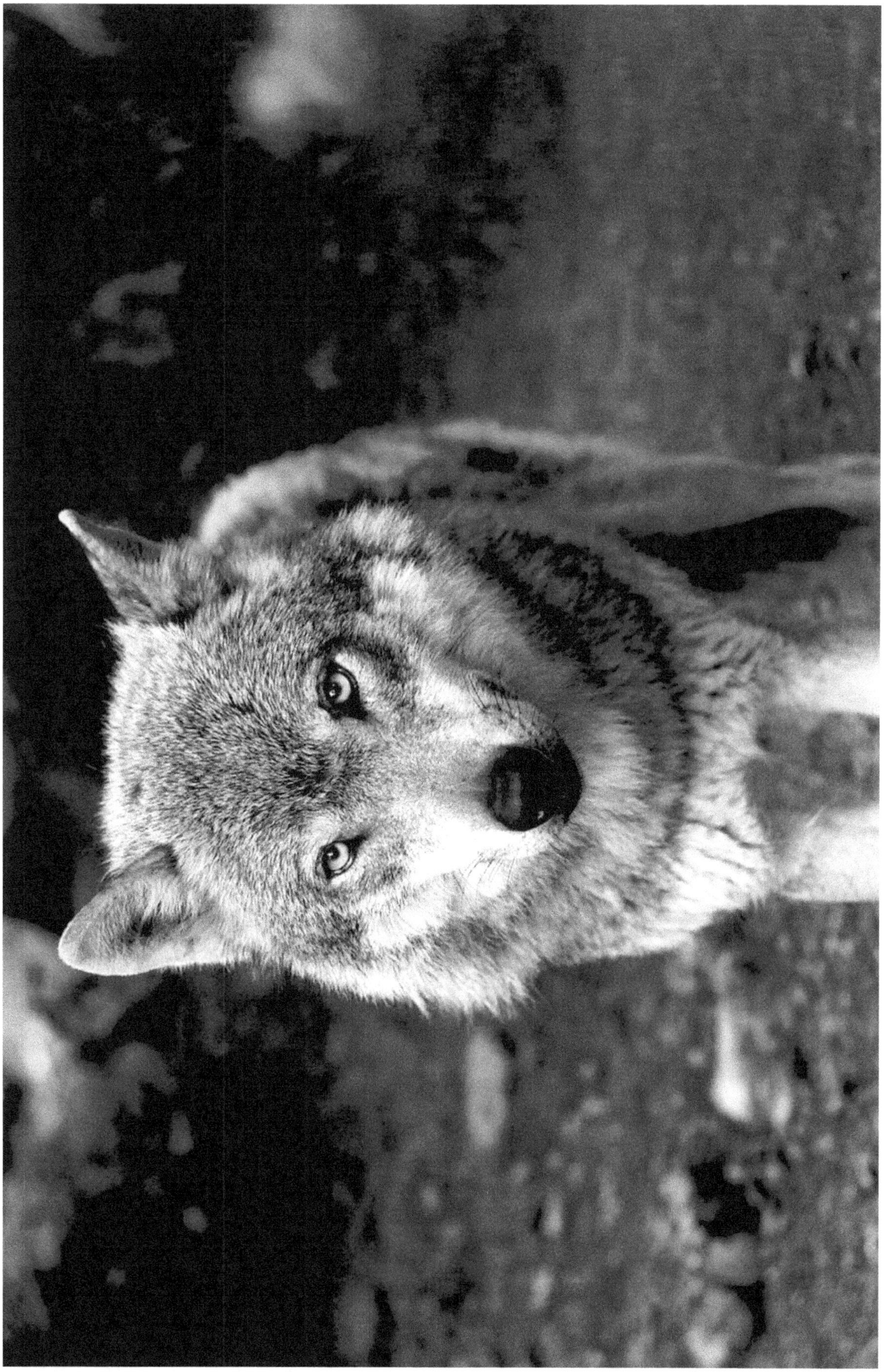